About

Jane _____ for 25 years.
For _____ business press,
for w_____nal collections
and interviewed designers from Gaultier to Galliano. She is
the co-author of *Fabulous Frocks* and *Elizabeth: Reigning in
Style*, also published by Pavilion. She has been writing for the
National Trust Books list for the last four years and was the
chief contributor to the *National Trust Book of the Countryside*.
Her other books include *Wild Food*, *Keeping Hens*, *Home-
Grown Fruit*, *Allotments*, *Herbs*, *Hedgerows & Wildlife* and
Mushrooms. Jane has produced two books linked to television
series: *Victorian Pharmacy* and *Britain by Bike*, which won
'Outdoor Book of the Year' at the 2011 Hay Festival. In her
spare time Jane is a keen amateur bird taxidermist.

the
art
of
Taxidermy

the
art
of
Taxidermy

Jane Eastoe

PAVILION

First published in the United Kingdom in 2012 by
PAVILION BOOKS
10 Southcombe Street,
London W14 0RA

An imprint of Anova Books Company Ltd

Text © Jane Eastoe, 2012
Foreword text © Polly Morgan, 2012
Design and layout © Anova Books, 2012
Photography © see Picture Credits on p.160

The moral right of the author has been asserted.

Commissioning editor: Emily Preece-Morrison
Project editor: Nina Sharman
Designers: Georgina Hewitt and Allan Sommerville
Special photography: Beth Evans
Stylist to special photography: Sophie Brown

ISBN: 978 1 86205 987 0

A CIP catalogue record for this book is available from the
British Library.

Colour reproduction by Rival Colour Ltd., UK
Printed and bound by Toppan Leefung Printing Ltd., China

www.anovabooks.com

10 9 8 7 6 5 4 3 2 1

Acknowledgements

I am deeply indebted to all the people who generously gave
up their time to talk to me, share their expertise, pass on their
contacts, patiently tolerate my endless queries and give me
tremendous encouragement. I must in particular thank the
following: artist Polly Morgan who kindly agreed to write the
thought-provoking foreword to this book and whose work
revived my long dormant interest in taxidermy; collector Errol
Fuller who gave up hours of his time and put up with much
inconvenience; sculptor and taxidermist Emily Mayer who
patiently explained her work; and taxidermist Carl Church
who gave me a display of the process as he passed on his
wisdom. Simon Wilson of Animal Animatronics explained
the use of taxidermy in contemporary media, and Andrew
Kitchener and Phil Howard from The Museum of Scotland
who detailed the scientific and educational significance of
both historic and contemporary taxidermy.

This book would not have been completed without the
support of my husband Eric, the cynical questions of my
children Teddy and Genevieve, and the superb subbing skills
of my daughter Florence. At Anova I am continually thankful
for the help and support of Polly Powell, Emily Preece-
Morrison, Charlotte Selby and the wonderful Nina Sharman.
I am also indebted to Georgina Hewitt and Allan
Sommerville for their superb design skills and endless
patience. Finally, I must thank David Leggett, who first
explained the mysteries of taxidermy to me and who inspired
me to write the book.

COVER IMAGE *For Sorrow* by Polly Morgan, 2007, shows
a magpie on an original Bakelite telephone. The work
explores Morgan's phobia of telephones – a conduit for bad
news – the warning magpie crouches on the cradle and
guards against the call being received.

PREVIOUS PAGE An uncased African guinea fowl of
unknown origin.

contents

Foreword by Polly Morgan **6**

Introduction **8**

CHAPTER ONE   The History of Taxidermy **12**

CHAPTER TWO   The Collectors **42**

CHAPTER THREE   Hunting Trophies **70**

CHAPTER FOUR   Realism **98**

CHAPTER FIVE   Cutting Edge **128**

APPENDIX   The Craft of Taxidermy **154**

Useful contacts **156**
Bibliography **159**
Picture credits **160**

foreword

On an almost daily basis I am asked the question, "Why taxidermy?" and, even after eight years, I struggle to find an adequate answer. The first thing that springs to mind is "Why not taxidermy?", as it seems odd to me that anyone should even wonder why I leapt at the chance to learn something that fulfills the fundamental needs to be creative and to understand the natural world.

One would think that the car fanatic who had never once lifted the bonnet to examine the engine was rather shallow. Yet the number of so-called "animal lovers" I've met who disdain taxidermy go unquestioned. I think this is because there are different degrees of animal love. There is the sentimental kind, where their vulnerability inspires a longing to protect and there is another, more sensuous kind, where the physicality of the creature is admired. The former I have always had in abundance while the latter, evident in my despair when yet another creature fled as I loomed in, had been lying dormant. It was a seed, germinated by taxidermy, that has blossomed into something more mature; a sincere respect for the animal form borne of a better understanding of how flesh and bone is structured to maximum effect, and how we see beauty in efficiency and reason.

Therefore, I baulk at the accusation that taxidermy doesn't treat an animal with "respect". Providing that the animal has been allowed to live and die as nature intended then this is respect enough for me.

To worry about what becomes of the remaining flesh and bone is to foist human codes onto a kingdom that frequently eats its own dead. The worst crime I see committed against animals by the taxidermist is to deprive a crow of a meal. Let's give respect to living animals by allowing them their freedom and to dead ones by doing our taxidermy as well as can be. This way we can enjoy them once they've finished with their bodies rather than cage them while they're still inhabited.

When I first became interested in the subject it was considered to be a "dying art" (no pun intended). I would disagree and say that it is an "evolving art". For so long taxidermists have been mimicking the natural habitat of their subject, with the occasional interruption from the likes of Walter Potter, seen as a lone eccentric and a less than skilled taxidermist. I hope that the work I do, and of other artists working in a similar vein, can ensure the survival of taxidermy by giving it a place in modern life. Just as photography put an end to much commissioning of painted portraits, so zoos, high definition video and cheap travel have seen the redundancy of many taxidermists, originally employed to educate us in natural history. Painting has survived, developing from figuration to abstraction, and so taxidermy must make similar shifts if it is to be considered the art I believe it is.

For too long taxidermy has undeservedly been the "guilty secret" of a few misunderstood practitioners and collectors, and at long last we have a book to herald its inclusion in popular culture.

Polly Morgan, 2012

RIGHT *Black Fever* by Polly Morgan, 2010, is a cluster of crow wings inspired by Eadweard Muybridge's photographic images of motion. Seven strata of wings gradually unfurl like a Mexican wave, demonstrating the rules of flight.

introduction

The skin, our largest organ, is the frontier between the inside and the outside of our bodies. It is one of our chief defining factors and yet it is unique; the pigmentation, the texture, the genetic characteristics, the hair, the fur, the freckles or the feathers mark out each species, each family, and indeed each individual creature. Skin is valuable; it is eaten, worn, upholstered and fetishistic. It is the raw material of taxidermy.

Taxidermy principally developed as a scientific and educational tool, a way of identifying and characterising species. It has moved in and out of fashion, been adored and reviled, and has symbolised both the best and worst of man's thirst for knowledge and tendency for ruthless exploitation. But taxidermy has evolved and developed into a modern art form, a means of self-expression and a respectful tribute to the beauty of the natural world.

The technical definition of the word taxidermy means to arrange a skin. It derives from the Greek roots *taxis* meaning arrangement, and *derma* meaning skin. A good taxidermist is part artist, part sculptor and part naturalist, but, and there is no getting away from it, taxidermists work with dead things. They skin and sculpt manikins to recreate and preserve an image of life – or death.

It is important at the outset to dispense with a time-honoured myth: that taxidermists kill their subjects. The laws governing taxidermy within the European Union are very strict. In the United Kingdom, for example, a General Licence, issued by Natural England, the body that advises the government on the natural environment, permits the taxidermy of most birds and mammals, excepting game and wildfowl during the closed season.

Separate sets of regulations govern those species contained within the various appendices

PREVIOUS PAGE *The Fall* by Polly Morgan, 2012, displays a fallen painted fibreglass tree, hollow, rotten and hung with seven plump piglets cast in silicone with a "flocked" velvety finish. The piglets gorge themselves from its "teats" like parasites. Sap runs, like milk, down their chins as they suck the life out of it. Birds, including an azure winged magpie, starlings and finches, are perched around the tree.

RIGHT A black-throated diver by John Cullingford of Durham looks like a piece of contemporary design, but actually dates circa 1890.

of the Convention on International Trade in Endangered Species of Wild Fauna and Flora (CITES) legislation. CITES is an agreement between countries that aims to ensure that the trade in specimens of wild animals and plants does not threaten their survival. It lays down strict rules as to the ownership of certain species, alive or dead, and governs commercial taxidermy practice, including its import and export.

CITES requires the individual certification of listed birds and mammals created after 1947, thereby proving their provenance; information including known history and cause and date of death must be detailed. All birds of prey are included within the CITES legislation, and each bird must be individually certificated. A taxidermist may only display, hire or sell such specimens when they have been approved by each EU Member State's licensing authority. In the UK, this licensing authority is the Animal Health Agency, which is part of the Department of the Environment, Farming and Rural Affairs (DEFRA). Taxidermists failing to comply with the letter of the law face severe penalties, including imprisonment.

Modern taxidermy, strictly governed by these rules, can be regarded as a form of recycling. Birds, beasts and fish die naturally and do not need to be killed for the purposes of taxidermy. As one taxidermist put it: "More things die naturally than we could ever utilise. We do not need to kill to obtain our raw material." Veterinary practices, zoos, wild-life parks, farmers and cat owners, whose pets bring "gifts", all deal with animal fatalities and are generally more than happy to see a corpse put to good use. The now defunct Mammals Trust UK, which kept a tally of road kill in the United Kingdom, estimated in 2008 that rabbits are the biggest mammal casualties with around 80,000 deaths a year. The badger, deer and grey squirrel populations each lose about 50,000 per year and the toll among pheasants is believed to be as high as 3,000,000. These fatalities, if not too badly damaged and suitably fresh, can potentially be utilised for the purposes of taxidermy.

In a world in which we are so insulated from death the basic reality of taxidermy can upset tender sensibilities. We disassociate ourselves from the essential link between a designer handbag and a cow chewing cud in the field. Those who squeal in horror at the prospect of a beautiful piece of taxidermy are generally ignorant of the reverential nature of the work. Taxidermy today is green, humane and respectful. It salutes the myriad wonders of the natural world. Its worst excesses should be considered in context for historical reference. It is time for taxidermy's renaissance.

LEFT A sloth by Rowland Ward in an all-glass case typifies his beautifully sculptural work which can be viewed successfully from every angle.

the history of taxidermy

"Our dead are never dead to us, until we have forgotten them."

GEORGE ELIOT (AUTHOR)

The oldest reputed piece of taxidermy in existence is suspended from the ceiling of a church in Lombardy, Italy. Its removal was documented in 1534, but it was later discovered unscathed residing in the roof in the eighteenth century.

Suspended from the ceiling of an Italian church is a record-breaking crocodile, put there around four and three-quarter centuries ago, it is the oldest piece of taxidermy in existence. Documentation relating to its removal from St Maria Annunziata, at Ponte Nossa in Lombardy, Italy in January 1534, proves that this remarkably life-like creature must be, at the very least, rather older than that date. This crocodile, later rediscovered squatting in the roof of said church, was put back on display in the eighteenth century. A number of Italian churches feature hanging crocodiles; the durability of the skin probably goes some way to explain why these particular specimens survived.

Crocodiles aside, the fact that so few early pieces exist is proof enough that taxidermists had not mastered their craft; namely, the successful preservation of a skin that is delicate, easily destroyed by insect infestation and damaged by both light and humidity. And, without verifiable pieces, it is impossible to determine precisely how long the art has been practiced.

Certainly initial attempts at bird and small mammal preservation involved drying specimens intact – innards and all – to create a fragrant lure for insects. As the drawbacks became apparent, specimens were skinned, cleaned and stuffed with aromatic packing, such as tobacco, hops and the herb wormwood, which has insecticidal properties. However, even this fragrant mix was not sufficient to deter insects and it was not until the 1740s, when the apothecary Jean-Baptiste Bécoeur (1718–77) developed a recipe for arsenical soap, that the problem was resolved. Unfortunately, Bécoeur's recipe was not disclosed until after his death. He had hoped to make some money out of it, but from the late-eighteenth century onwards taxidermists, or "stuffers" as they were then known, already had the means to efficiently preserve bird skins.

Nevertheless, a few venerable specimens have survived from around 1600 onwards, notably prized horses or dogs: Archduke Albert's horse, which was hit by a musket ball at the Battle of Nieuport in 1600, resides in The Museum of the Army in Brussels. The beast was preserved, complete with its heroic wound, for posterity. The prize steed of the Swedish King Gustav Adolphus, which was shot from beneath him at Ingolstadt, Bavaria in 1632, during the course of the Thirty Years War, suffered the indignity of being skinned, mounted and exhibited as a war trophy by the German opposition. It is reputed to neigh whenever war is imminent – last heard in 1939 – and can still be seen in the town museum.

The oldest existing stuffed bird is believed to be an African Grey Parrot which belonged to Frances

LEFT King Gustav Adolphus' horse was shot from beneath him in a battle at Ingolstadt, Bavaria in 1632 and was exhibited as a war trophy by the German opposition. It can still be seen at the Ingolstadt town museum.

Stuart, the Duchess of Richmond and mistress to King Charles II. The bird, of which she was inordinately fond, can still be seen in Westminster Abbey Museum, perched next to a life size wax effigy of the Duchess herself. She requested that the bird be preserved after its death – she died first in 1702, the parrot a short while later.

Aside from the preservation of the prized pets of the rich and famous there was little need for taxidermy. When animals died their skins were put to good use for clothing, footwear and bedding and so on. Home decoration was scarcely significant save for the very wealthy, and even then it was skulls and antlers that were put on display as hunting trophies.

The real interest in taxidermy developed as a result of exploration in the sixteenth and seventeenth centuries. The discoveries of new species of flora and fauna were of immense fascination, but experience proved that few survived removal from their natural habitat let alone a long sea trip. While butterflies, beetles, insects and seashells were relatively easy to preserve, birds and mammals presented more of a problem and taxidermy offered a solution. Robert Boyle discovered that animals could be preserved in alcohol in 1664, offering a means by which specimens could remain intact until such time as they could be put in the hands of a taxidermist. Study skins were collected by the thousand to show the minute variations within a species. The preservation of the study skin was often sufficient in itself for, without any visual reference material, the production of a lifelike model through taxidermy was nigh on impossible, nevertheless, some taxidermists gave it their best shot.

These early specimens, acquired by royalty, wealthy collectors and scholars were displayed in Cabinets of Curiosities, a collection of ephemera that reflected a growing scientific interest in the wonders of the natural world. A preserved crocodile could rub shoulders with a piece of coral, some seashells, a giant seed, a two-headed lamb, an ostrich egg or the skin of a bird of paradise. It is these early collections that formed the basic stock of many early museums.

It was not until the Swedish botanist, Carl Linnaeus (1707–78), set himself the business of undertaking the biological classification of all life on earth – animal, vegetable and mineral – using his own system of binomial nomenclature (two names), that there was any serious reference material. Without reference, scientists could not ascertain whether a new specimen had been previously identified or if it was indeed an entirely new species, a genetic abnormality or indeed a fake.

RIGHT A cabinet of curiosities on display at Malplaquet House, London, in a contemporary tribute to the compulsive collecting of bygone eras.

And with all manner of marvellous creatures being touted around, cynics must surely have concluded that not everything came from nature.

As a young student Linnaeus was shown what was purported to be a preserved seven-headed hydra, he quickly concluded that it was a chimera composed of snake and weasel skins. When the platypus was first discovered in Australia in 1798, Captain John Hunter, the second Governor of New South Wales, despatched the skin to Britain along with an accompanying sketch. It looked so improbable that sceptics initially believed it was a hoax and that a duck's beak had been sewn onto a beaver type animal. But then it was not unknown for taxidermists to create mythical creatures, such as dragons, unicorns, griffins and mermaids, which would be exhibited at sideshows, so perhaps such cynicism was understandable. By the late eighteenth century taxidermy was becoming increasingly common.

The public interest in natural history was phenomenal, and must be considered in context. The limited scientific understanding of the natural world expanded rapidly in the eighteenth and nineteenth centuries, the foundations of modern biology were being developed and Darwin's publication, *On the Origin of the Species*, in 1859, caused immense controversy. There were no photographic images of these extraordinary new species of flora and fauna and certainly no film footage. Even indigenous species were of interest for there were no binoculars to allow for close perusal, but the more exotic birds and animals caused a sensation. And even artists specialising in bird illustration utilised taxidermy to assist them, for their subjects simply would not remain still. Painter and ornithologist John James Audubon (1785–1851) practised taxidermy to help him produce his exquisite bird illustrations, and even as late as 1914 the legendary bird illustrator, Archibald Thorburn, used skins as reference.

Early museums utilised taxidermy to draw crowds who were prepared to pay handsomely to view the spectacular wonders of the natural world. The Leverian Museum in London was home to a huge attraction; thousands of mammals, fish, birds and insects brought back by no lesser person than Captain Cook from his Voyages of Exploration (1772–79). William Bullock's Museum boasted 4,000 curiosities that were exhibited in Liverpool and London to a curious public. The introduction to *The Companion to Bullock's Museum*, published in 1813, stated: "Various animals, such as the Lofty Giraffe, the Lion, the Elephant, the Rhinoceros etc., are exhibited as ranging in their native wilds and forests …". The British Museum

LEFT A pair of Saki monkeys from South America, circa 1830, one stuffed as in life, the other to resemble a small hairy man by Charles Waterton who wrote *Waterton's Wanderings in South America*, one of the most successful travel books of the nineteenth century. Note the monkey skull in the bottom of the case.

ABOVE An engraving of magpies by Robert Havell from
John James Audubon's book, *The Birds of America*, popularly
regarded as one of the finest ornithological works. Audubon
utilised taxidermy and bird skins in his own illustrations.

RIGHT A selection of tropical birds, mostly South
American, circa 1880. The glass dome is unusually
constructed utilising three pieces of glass from
traditionally shaped domes.

installed its first bird group in 1877 and it was approximately ten more years before a bird exhibit appeared in the American Museum of Natural History (AMNH).

The Great Exhibition in 1851 included a number of taxidermy exhibits. Herman Ploucquet, a German taxidermist, exhibited anthropomorphic taxidermy, animals engaged in human activity. The *Morning Chronicle* of 12 August 1851 noted that Ploucquet's exhibits were: "one of the most crowded points of the Exhibition". The Great Exhibition, which attracted some six million visitors, is generally held to be the turning point for taxidermy as many of the displays were of a high technical standard and utilised great artistry in scenes and tableaux that, compared to the simply posed species on display in museums, provoked great excitement. The art was now about so much more than the successful preservation of the skin, genuine artistry was required to produce life-like models and techniques in moulding and sculpting body forms.

London taxidermist, John Gould, opted not to show at The Great Exhibition, but instead put on display twenty-four elaborate cases of humming-birds in the Zoological Gardens in Regents Park. He charged visitors sixpence to enter and is reputed to have attracted 75,000 visitors.

RIGHT Herman Ploucquet, a taxidermist at The Royal Museum of Stuttgart, showed his work at the Great Exhibition at Crystal Palace in 1851 and inspired many imitators. Queen Victoria recorded in her diary that his work was "marvellous".

Public interest grew and retailers such as Deyrolle in Paris, one of the most famous purveyors of taxidermy and natural history curiosities in the world, opened its doors in 1831. Royal Warrant holder, Rowland Ward (1848–1912), whose shop in London's Piccadilly was known as "The Jungle", catered to this new trend in interior décor offering everything from hunting trophies, to the black bear calling card holder, the elephant-foot umbrella stand, or intricate displays of butterflies. Artistic arrangements of bird species were hugely popular, although taxidermists exhibited scant regard for ornithological accuracy.

Perhaps the Victorians embraced the art of taxidermy so enthusiastically because of their morbid fascination with death. They turned death and mourning into a virtual fetish – although when one considers that childhood mortality was shockingly high and the average life span for middle class males was forty-four years, and just twenty-six years for the working classes, this is perhaps understandable. They took death masks of their dear departed and wore locks of their hair.

LEFT Deyrolle still sells taxidermy today. The shop was almost destroyed by a fire caused by a short circuit in 2008, ninety per cent of its stock was lost. Donations from collectors and museums and a massive fund raising exercise helped to re-establish the business.

OVERLEAF A group of young girls gaze in wonder at a taxidermy elephant in The Natural History Museum, London in 1931.

"The Victorians turned death and mourning into a virtual fetish …"

Queen Victoria famously mourned Prince Albert with a zealous fervour; servants were required to bring up hot water for his shaving cup long after his death and the glass from which he took his last dose of medicine remained by his bed for four decades.

Next to such morbidity, cases containing literally hundreds of humming birds displaying their plumage seemed positively joyful. And perhaps by way of contrast to everyday life, anything brightly coloured was particularly popular. In defence of taxidermy, the fashion for feathers, principally in millinery, accounted for the mass import and death of many more birds. Pets were also preserved; Charles Dickens had his pet raven Grip, who featured in *Barnaby Rudge*, stuffed after it died in 1841, it now resides with a collector in the United States.

Early museums displayed taxidermy in serried ranks for the purposes of comparative morphology. However, as the nineteenth century moved towards its close, taxidermists were increasingly interested in recreating precise habitats, a trend that gradually altered the thinking in museums and resulted in the introduction of fabulous dioramas of everything, from birds on their nests to sweeping vistas of the African plains, dotted with elephant and giraffe. Rowland Ward (1848–1912) in Britain and Carl (or Clarence) Akeley (1864–1926) in the United States both sought to produce the most life-like representations possible and used new techniques in mammal taxidermy.

LEFT A case of humming-birds by Ashmead, circa 1850, typifies Victorian passionate excess turning taxidermy into a sculptural design form. There are in excess of 300 birds in the giant case but it is impossible to count them precisely.

ABOVE The mythical jackalope of North American folklore, photographed here in 1987 in a novelty shop in Silverton, Colorado, was commonly recreated by combining the body of a jack-rabbit with the horns of an antelope.

RIGHT This nineteenth century case of miniature dogs, of unknown origin, features black and tan terriers bred by McDouglas Holman from his bitch Busy Body – five out of a litter of nine survived. It is likely that these were stillborn puppies stuffed to look like adult miniatures.

The latest techniques used by Ward and Akeley involved sculpting the bodies in clay to produce a realistic musculature from which moulds could be taken and manikins produced, initially using papier mâché, to produce a strong, but light form. In the home, taxidermy specimens were popped into cases, with delicately painted backdrops amid a jumble of plant life.

But not all taxidermy moved in the same direction. Walter Potter (1835-1918) is reputed to have seen Ploucquet's anthropomorphic taxidermy at the Great Exhibition and been inspired to utilise his talents to create scenic taxidermy. As his collection grew he created his own museum in Bramber, Sussex, where he displayed his work along with a selection of general ephemera; Siamese twin pigs in alcohol, or the jawbone of an ass. His first and most famous piece of work was to create a tableau that showed the death of Cock Robin, of nursery rhyme fame, which he worked on in his spare time over seven years and that features ninety-eight different bird species. But he also depicted guinea pigs playing cricket, rabbits in a village school, kittens enjoying a tea party, and toads exercising – an automated tableau that was activated by putting a penny in the slot.

Potter's museum opened its doors in 1880 and was so popular that, despite an increasingly sophisticated consumer, it remained open for just under a century, finally closing for good in 1972. The contents were moved to a museum in Brighton and then later to Jamaica Inn, in Cornwall; it is estimated that over the years Potter's taxidermy was viewed by millions of people. His collection was finally broken up and sold as individual pieces in 2003 for £500,000. Few would argue that Potter, who was self-taught, was a taxidermist of any great skill; bodies are overstuffed and the eyes are, frankly, disturbing, but then again Potter was not intending to reproduce nature. Whether one views his work as charming or demeaning to the animals, it depicts, is very much a matter of personal taste, it is certainly a curious piece of historical kitsch. Perhaps Potter was merely doing with taxidermy what Walt Disney later did, rather more successfully, with cartoons.

While Rowland Ward was developing his diorama for the collector Major Percy Horace Gordon Powell-Cotton (1866–1940) at Quex Park, near Birchington in Kent, Carl Akeley was working on taxidermy projects of a similar scale in the United States. He started his career by stuffing a neighbour's pet canary and worked up from there to Jumbo, the world's biggest African elephant owned and shown by showman P. T. Barnum.

PREVIOUS PAGE A close-up of a Rowland Ward diorama from Quex Park in Birchington, Kent is a perfect example of the famous taxidermist's extraordinary work. The attention to detail, incorporating all manner of flora and fauna in each scene, is extraordinary.

LEFT A perfect example of a taxidermist creating a miniature world, here a cased hare by Peter Spicer & Son of Leamington Spa, 1921.

Jumbo was the first project where Akeley was given his head. He built a manikin to scale, covered it with pliant strips of wood to imitate the elephant's musculature and then covered this in putty that he could carve. His work was complicated by the fact that Barnum had asked him to make the elephant even bigger in death than it had been in life. The end result caused a sensation, it was said to be very life-like and was exhibited at The Powers Building in Rochester. P. T. Barnum also displayed "the Feejee mermaid", which seamlessly combined the head and body of a monkey with the tail of a large fish; Barnum was canny enough to show it in a glass case making close inspection difficult.

Akeley wound up, via the Milwaukee Public Museum and the Columbian Museum of Chicago, as taxidermist to the American Museum of Natural History. His aim was always to show the animals as realistically as possible in their natural habitat. He convinced the museums of the worth of the enterprise by emphasising that it would be sure to attract big crowds. His Muskrat diorama, installed in 1890, still attracts visitors today. Akeley was not the first to show animals within a setting, but he was perhaps the first to do it so well, with such artistry and commitment to composition. His work culminated in the Akeley Hall of African Mammals at the American Museum of Natural History.

Akeley, like Powell-Cotton, went on many "collecting" expeditions for each of the museums he worked for. According to Dave Madden, in *The Authentic Animal*, in the course of five collecting trips to Africa he shot: "328 various forms of antelope (e.g., gazelles, dik-diks, duikers, impalas, hartebeests, gemsboks), 103 rodents, 27 monkeys, 20 elephants, 16 lions, 13 warthogs, 12 jackals, 9 gorillas, 8 baboons, 6 buffalo, 6 zebras, 5 donkeys, 3 cheetahs, 3 hippos, 2 rhinoceros, 2 giraffes, 2 leopards and a porcupine." In Akeley's own memoir, *In Brightest Africa*, he recalls a life and death struggle with a leopard that charged him after he had shot it. He ended up suffocating the leopard by pushing his fist down her throat – she had his arm in her jaws at the time – and he freely admits that not only was it a fight to the death, but also a close run thing which one of the two would survive. The leopard was not alone in its intent; an elephant had a good crack at trying to crush the breath out of Akeley in 1910.

Despite the fact that Akeley killed many mammals and birds in the name of science, he did, towards the end of his career understand the damage that hunting caused and went some way to making atonement. Travelling through the

RIGHT Two small boys are entranced by Walter Potter's piece *The Village School* at his museum in Bramber, Sussex in 1950, some 32 years after the death of its whimsical creator.

Congo in 1921 en route to Uganda to hunt for mountain gorilla specimens, which had only been described in scientific literature as recently as 1903, he wrote: "I doubt if the entire gorilla population will exceed fifty individuals. It will be a very simple matter to exterminate them." He instigated work in setting up a national park to protect the gorilla's habitat to ensure no more lost their lives to hunters.

Zoologist and conservationist William Temple Hornaday (1854–1937) was another mover and shaker in the world of taxidermy. He worked for Ward's Natural Science Establishment, who supplied taxidermy specimens to museums. Hornaday went on a specimen hunting trip on behalf of Ward's, as a result of which he created a display of two orang-utans, named "The Fight in the Tree-Tops", and after which he was appointed chief taxidermist at the Smithsonian Museum in Washington, D.C. He heard that the American bison were being decimated and though troubled by the morality of the exercise went to Montana to hunt for several specimens. Hornaday was so appalled by the skeletal remains of so many slaughtered bison that he highlighted their plight and his work resulted in the creation of federally protected bison ranges in the American northwest. His famous bison display can still be seen today at

RIGHT Workmen ease a 4.6m (15ft) stuffed giraffe onto its side to enable it to fit through the doors of the Natural History Museum, London where it was to be exhibited, in 1959.

the Museum of The Northern Great Plains in Fort Benton, Montana. Hornaday later developed the New York Zoological Park, now known as the Bronx Zoo.

A change of attitude began to emerge after the First World War. Perhaps it was the advent of the movies, or the new clean cut lines of contemporary design that swept the cluttered and gloomy Victorian décor aside. Taxidermy began to be regarded as a relic of nineteenth century colonialism. Country homes might boast hunting trophies, but elsewhere taxidermy did not sit comfortably in modern interiors – the number of working taxidermists steadily declined.

By the 1950s and 1960s taxidermy was seen as politically incorrect and many museums started to remove their taxidermy collections, some were sold, some broken up, others sit in storage. Natural history programmes, which beamed the glories of the natural world into the home, reinforced the notion that taxidermy was an outdated art. Who needed to see a static mount when the real thing could be seen in its natural habitat? Moreover, as public interest in animal welfare increased, the craft of taxidermy became tainted by association. The future of taxidermy hung in the balance.

LEFT A group of bison collected and mounted by William Temple Hornaday between 1886 and 1887 in the South Hall of the U.S. National Museum, later known as the Arts and Industries Building. Hornaday highlighted the plight of the bison resulting in the creation of a national park.

LEFT A rare example of a style of French taxidermy, circa 1900, by Ledot, with a ptarmigan framed and mounted under curved glass.

ABOVE A cape pigeon in the same French style, circa 1880, is arranged to fit its frame. This type of taxidermy was commonly kept in kitchens.

CHAPTER TWO

the collectors

"From my rotting body,
flowers shall grow and
I am in them and
that is eternity."

EDVARD MUNCH (ARTIST)

A taxidermy display of Golden Beetles (*Plusiotis optima*)
shows the range of colour diversity in a collection at the
National Biodiversity Institute in San José, Costa Rica.

genetic anomalies such as albinos – and scoured the world for exotic new specimens of birds and mammals. Fortunes were spent in their cause; Major Powell-Cotton embarked on a safari to British East Africa in 1905 to hunt for specimens, lasting almost three years and costing him £4,000, which equates to around £1.5 million today.

The all-pervading atmosphere of mystery and romance that their extraordinary collections imbued intoxicated these gentlemen. Their homes were a testament to their obsession with the natural world and their passion for compulsive collecting, all displayed in elegant disorder. Contemporary interiors that reflect the days of the great collectors mark a major shift in interior design, with a move away from minimalist living in favour of a chaotic mix of *objet d'art* that transforms ordinary rooms into gothic palaces of wonder.

Tea trader Frederick Horniman's (1835–1906) home was a prime example. He collected all manner of interesting ephemera from far-flung lands until his collections accumulated to such a degree that his wife is reputed to have said, "either the collection goes or we do". The impasse was solved by Horniman buying another house close by for the family and throwing open the original as a museum in 1890. The Horniman museum in South London still welcomes visitors.

The early collectors of taxidermy were natural historians, fired with enthusiasm for a subject area that was at the forefront of scientific development and understanding; it was a diverting pastime for wealthy gentleman. They classified and catalogued every known indigenous species – delighting in any

ABOVE Major Powell-Cotton, seen here with Dinka tribesmen in Sudan in 1932, spent millions in a series of twenty-eight collecting expeditions. He was a pioneer in the exhibition of larger mammals in their natural habitat in massive dioramas.

RIGHT Powell-Cotton leads a safari in British East Africa in 1901, seen here crossing the Kikuyu Bridge.

ABOVE A collection of taxidermy from the Natural History Gallery of the Horniman Museum in 1913. Most of the large mammals were removed from the collection in 1948.

RIGHT A walrus from Hudson Bay, Canada mounted in the late 1800s by taxidermists who had little knowledge of the anatomy of the creature. This overstuffed specimen was first shown in the Colonial and Indian Exhibition, London in 1886 and joined the Horniman Collection in the early 1890s. It can still be seen today.

The thirteenth Earl of Derby, Edward Smith Stanley (1775–1851) was one of the earliest gentleman collectors. Fascinated by natural history he acquired over one hundred mounted birds from the Leverian Museum sale in 1806 alone. He later commissioned collectors to travel the world despatching specimens to him. By his death in 1851 his collection encompassed every major group of animals and birds and he bequeathed some 20,000 birds and mammals to the people of Liverpool, for a "nominal" £20,000, a sum considerably lower than the value of the collection. Incidentally, he also collected living animals; there were 1,272 birds and 345 mammals at Knowsley at his death. The Derby Museum opened in Liverpool in 1853, showing a mere fraction of Lord Derby's bequest and even so managed to attract 157,861 visitors in just seven months – the building was too small to accommodate the crowds. A number of his specimens are now extinct, including the Long-tailed Hopping Mouse, the Swamp Hen, the Paradise Parrot and the Himalayan Mountain Quail.

Hans Sloane's collection, which later became the foundation of the Natural History Museum in London, is described by the Swede, Peter Kalm, in his *Account of a Visit to England*, written in 1748: "various stuffed birds and fish, where the birds often stood fast on small bits of board as naturally as if they still lived". He also cites "the stuffed skin of a camel, an African many striped ass, humming birds set in their nests and a collection of snakes, lizards, fishes, birds, caterpillars, insects and small four-footed animals etc., all put in *spiritu vin* in bottles, and well preserved".

These gentlemen were not alone, collectors were acquiring specimens all over the western world, and many formed the basis of museum collections, although their gift to posterity was not all it may have appeared. Hans Sloane's collection did not survive so well. William Swainson wrote in his 1840 book *Taxidermy*: "In the British Museum there are, it is true, vast numbers of specimens, but the majority are so old and faded that two thirds might be cast out with much advantage."

The substitution of old models for fresh new ones continues in museums today, and seems to have been common practice even by the late-eighteenth century. The greatest loss perhaps was that of a mounted dodo, originally from the Tradescant Collection in London and latterly in the Ashmolean Collection in Oxford. It was burnt in 1755 when the museum decided to get rid of some tired examples – thus depriving science of one of the last remaining specimens – the dodo is thought to have been extinct by the 1680s.

LEFT This budgerigar chick was the first ever budgie to be hatched in Britain in the 13th Lord Derby's aviaries at Knowsley Hall in 1848. It died aged just three weeks old, was stuffed, and can be seen today at the new waterfront Museum of Liverpool.

OVERLEAF Collector Edward Booth founded the Booth Natural History Museum in 1874. It is home to over three-quarter of a million specimens with a focus on birds, butterflies, fossils, bones and skeletons.

It is, however, worth noting that not all skins deteriorated. The Museum of Edinburgh still has a specimen of *Manis crassicaudata* – or scaly ant-eater – collected by David Samwell, the surgeon on Captain Cook's third and final expedition (1776–80), which came to them via the sale of the contents of William Bullock's Museum.

Meanwhile the gentlemen collectors continued to gather specimens: naturalist Edward Booth (1840–90) was a fanatical ornithologist, determined to source a specimen of every British bird. His resulting collection, including 650 types of butterfly, is still on display in Brighton in the Booth Natural History Museum that he opened in 1874 and which contains three quarters of a million specimens. Booth is famous for commissioning many beautiful bird dioramas.

The splendidly named eccentric, Sir Vauncey Harpur-Crewe (1846–1924), of Calke Abbey, was a mite obsessive about bird taxidermy, although his interest also extended to moths and butterflies. By his death he had amassed several thousand cases, devoting all his attentions to this passion, while his house fell apart around him. Some of the collection was sold to pay death duties. The National Trust acquired the house and what remained of his extraordinary collection. Harpur-Crewe, like many collectors, was a big personality;

he was so frightened of fire – many taxidermy collections were destroyed by flames – that his household was banned from smoking, his daughter Airmyne broke the rule and was banished, never to return to Calke.

The elaborately named Percy Horace Gordon Powell-Cotton was a collector, hunter and naturalist. In twenty-eight trips, mostly in Africa, between 1887 and 1939 he gathered an astonishing number of specimens, all of which were tagged and logged, with their weight, measurement and precise location recorded in latitude and longitude. He shot his specimens himself, and some might argue that as such, he was in essence a game hunter. However, Powell-Cotton was motivated by his interest in natural history and through his work he has left an astonishing legacy, commissioning many thousands of taxidermy pieces.

After a twenty month trip to Africa, Powell-Cotton wrote a book, snappily titled, *In Unknown Africa: A Narrative of Twenty Months Travel and Sport in Unknown Lands and Among New Tribes*, published in 1904, in which he states:

As far as I know at present the most interesting result of the journey, from the point of view of the general public, is the group of giraffe at the Natural History Museum. To the best of my

OVERLEAF The last of the mammal galleries, completed in 1947, at Quex Park features animals from the African savannah, a selection of monkeys and apes of Africa, an Indian forest by moonlight and a range of scenes from Zululand, Ethiopia and North Africa. Some of the skins had been in storage for forty years.

RIGHT A view of taxidermy enthusiast Sir Vauncey Harpur-Crewe's bedroom at Calke Abbey. The property, now in the hands of the National Trust, has been preserved and is a perfect example of the décor and lifestyle of the mid-nineteenth century collector.

belief adult males have only been set up in two European museums. When the rest of the zoological trophies have been examined, it is possible that another new sub-species or two may be found. In any case the series of zebra, Hueglin's, Grant's, bushbuck and guereza should throw fresh light on the distribution of those animals. The trip has also proved that the lesser kudu has a far wider range than was formerly supposed … As has already been shown if I had been treated in a less niggardly and suspicious spirit, my range would have been more extensive, and the National Collection would have reaped a larger harvest. The wasted opportunities and the disappointment are mine, but the loss to museums and to the wider scientific knowledge of this country affects far wider interests."

At his home, Quex Park near Birchington in Kent, Powell-Cotton built a museum where, utilising the considerable skills of taxidermist Rowland Ward, he organised the creation of some of the first and finest dioramas. By all accounts he was a demanding customer and the resulting dioramas, which can still be seen at the museum, are extraordinary works of art on a grand scale, albeit rather more crowded than might occur in reality, with various species in one location. The Major himself bagged all the specimens, save a few shot by other family members. Here the public can find gorillas, chimpanzees, tigers, leopards, giraffe, ibex, oryx, gazelle, buffalo, bongo, elephant and rhinoceros. Powell-Cotton learned first-hand that hunting for specimens was a dangerous business: one lion made a spirited attempt to kill him after being shot at. Fortunately for the Major, it later transpired that the bullet had broken the lion's jaw, so it could only maul him with its claws – the rips can still be seen on his safari suit at Quex Park. The same lion is immortalised in a dramatic piece of taxidermy showing a fight to the death with a buffalo.

Among the vegetation, typical but not actual botanical specimens, butterflies and insects can be seen; the attention to detail is impeccable. Not on view to the public is the rest of his irreplaceable collection, skulls, bones and skins, all catalogued and available for reference and increasingly utilised by the scientific community for DNA analysis.

The zoologist Baron Walter Rothschild (1868–1937) is perhaps one of the best-known collectors. As a small child he watched a taxidermist at work and almost immediately declared his intention to build a museum, which he dutifully did, opening it to the public in 1892, though doubtless having a wealthy financier as a father helped his quest. The museum attracted some 30,000 visitors a year.

LEFT A Rowland Ward lion head, date unknown. Above it is a rare Victorian case of an A. R. Wallace Standard-wing Bird of Paradise. Ward, a skilled artist and sculptor, created a tableau, utilising over one hundred specimens, for the Colonial and Indian Exhibition of 1886 which attracted over five and a half million visitors and established his reputation.

"Rothschild formed the largest zoological collection ever amassed by a private individual."

Baron Walter Rothschild embarked on some expeditions personally, and in a letter dated 22 July 1908, he describes a night in France:

We set up the lamp at 8.15 & up to 8.45 we had caught our usual 80–100 but at 8.45 came with a rush & Dr J Harmon and I could not cope with it all in spite of having 7 Cyanide bottles, over 200 glass boxes and a large chloroform tin. The gauze cage around the lamp which is 1 metre [3 ft] long by ¾ metre [2½ ft] broad and ¾ metre [2½ ft] high was covered on all sides with a seething struggling mass of moths such as I suppose was never seen before in Europe.

To give some idea of the scale of the collection Rothschild had 2,000 complete mounted mammals, 2,400 mounted birds, 680 reptiles, 914 fishes and a representative collection of invertebrates. He also had 1,400 mammal skins and skulls, 300,000 bird skins, 200,000 birds' eggs, 300 dried reptiles, 2¼ million Lepidoptera and 300,00 beetles. Rothschild sold the bulk of his 280,000-bird skin collection to the American Museum of Natural History for $225,000, a little under a dollar a skin, to pay off a blackmailer. When the sale was made public – Walter's family only learned of it through newspaper reports – ornithologist David Bannerman observed that the loss of the skins "was an epoch making event

PREVIOUS PAGE The eccentric collector Walter Rothschild first brought zebras to Tring in 1894. He broke them in and though never very reliable, once drove them down Piccadilly to Buckingham Palace where Princess Alexandra attempted to pat them.

RIGHT Polar bears don't smile, but this specimen from the Natural History Museum at Tring, and originally part of Sir Walter Rothschild's collection, is showing an amiable face to the world.

which closes what had probably been the most progressive chapter British Ornithology had ever seen". Nevertheless, the bulk of Rothschild's collection is preserved and still open to the public in its original setting at the Natural History Museum, Tring, Hertfordshire where 2,000 specimens of birds alone – including every British bird – more than any other museum in the world, can be seen.

Tring is also home to a startling, but rather splendid collection of taxidermy canines, including champion greyhounds such as the legendary Mick the Miller (1926–38), who won forty-six of his sixty-one races including the Greyhound Derby twice. Taxidermist Rowland Ward worked on many of these dogs, which were all approved by judges as typical of their breed. There is even a pair of dressed fleas from Mexico.

The life of the collector did not always run smoothly as Rothschild discovered. Following a visit by a Dr Cyril Cunningham, the caretaker of the museum noticed that a number of type specimens were missing, on rushing out to the street to see if Dr Cunningham's car was still in the vicinity, he found nothing but a pile of type labels in the gutter, indicating that the skins had been stolen. Rothschild who was distraught at the news, took the advice of his sister-in-law, Rozsika,

LEFT Mick the Miller (1926–38) was a champion greyhound idolised by millions of British greyhound racegoers. His owners had him stuffed after his death as a tribute to his great career. He now resides in the Natural History Museum at Tring.

and wrote to Cunningham advising him that the King of Bulgaria, a keen ornithologist, was coming to visit and had asked to see all type specimens. He would, therefore, be most grateful if Cunningham could return all of the specimens that he had been "lent". The specimens were promptly returned!

Collectors who commission still exist, often with a passionate attachment to a particular species or type of bird or mammal, but they are atypical compared to past collectors. However, the enthusiasm for collecting historical pieces is on the rise. Collector, artist and author Errol Fuller has witnessed the huge increase in interest in taxidermy curios that he used to bid for with little or no competition. Fuller reckons he now has in excess of 500 cases of taxidermy and maintains that his interest is, in part, a primitive instinct to preserve life after death: " if you stuff a dead thing to look as though it is alive, then surely that is some kind of rage against the fact that we are all going to die", he observes. He derives great pleasure from being able to examine specimens that one could never, under normal circumstances, get near to: "but in addition I like the little fantasy worlds, the simulated scenes that the Victorian taxidermists created, they are things of great mystery." Fuller started collecting as a child:

The first thing I can remember buying was a kingfisher from a jumble sale. But I quickly discovered that junk shops and antique shops had things too and for not much more money. Taxidermy was so unfashionable that I could buy bits for sixpence. I used to help shop-owners; sweep their floors or look after business while they had lunch, and in return I would get a wonderful glass dome of birds that they had no real prospect of selling. It shaped my life; there I was sitting in a council house in South London with things that once upon a time were a rich man's game.

"To my mind the golden age of Natural History collection is over and rightly so," Fuller notes, "I don't want things if they are new and have been killed for the purposes of science or taxidermy and I am not interested in hunting. These things were probably all hunted, but they were all hunted before I was born. I compare it to an executioner's axe, it did something terrible, but it still has historic value."

LEFT A platypus of unknown date and origin resides in its own tiny world. When the species was first encountered in Australia in 1798 a sketch and pelt was sent back to Britain where scientists decreed it an improbable taxidermy hoax.

RIGHT Maunsel House, a 13th century manor house
in Somerset, epitomises the traditional country house
interior with walls littered with hunting trophies,
notably fox heads and fish.

OVERLEAF Taxidermy is damaged by extremes of heat,
sunlight and humidity, however, this does not always deter
enthusiasts from utilising every spare inch of space; here
a bathroom is an unlikely home to a range of specimens.

CHAPTER THREE

hunting trophies

" … there may well be more art in a stuffed pike than a dead sheep."

BRIAN SEWELL (ART CRITIC)

A wall of kudu heads in a taxidermy shop in Namibia. The kudu's exquisite horns, which can reach 1.8m (6ft), made it a trophy target for hunters.

To write about taxidermy and ignore the existence of hunting trophies is akin to trying to ignore the stuffed elephant in the room. Of all forms of taxidermy it is these specimens that sit most uncomfortably with our modern sensibilities. Hunting is part of our communal history and although the hunter-gatherer lifestyle continues to this day in some communities, most societies moved towards farming after prehistoric times. As the necessity of hunting for survival became, theoretically at least, redundant, so the concept of hunting for sport was born. To kill merely for the thrill of it and to record that moment for posterity by stuffing your kill, has become the unacceptable face of taxidermy – despite hunters arguing that preserving a kill is a mark of respect. And whether one approves of "the sport" or not, hunting game can be legally undertaken all over the world; though the necessity for the trophy may seem less pertinent now than it did in the eighteenth and nineteenth centuries when the only way to record a kill was to preserve it.

Bird and animal representation has always been utilised by man, from pre-historic cave paintings, through decorative belt buckles, sword hilts, shields and helmets, as well as in woodcarving in furniture. Animals feature in coats of arms on shields: antlers symbolise strength and fortitude;

RIGHT Bow hunters use bow and arrow to hunt their prey. Here a contemporary bow hunter's trophy room is packed with kills.

"Rowland Ward was regarded by many as the finest British historical taxidermist of his time."

the lion bravery, strength, ferocity and valour; and the snake wisdom and, similarly, trophy shields send coded messages. Rowland Ward was one of the earliest taxidermists to utilise the shield for trophy heads from 1880, and Peter Spicer and Sons were famous for fox masks.

The nineteenth and early twentieth centuries were the "golden days" of trophy hunting. A trophy emphatically proved that you had caught the biggest fish, shot the deer with the heaviest antlers, netted the rarest butterfly or bagged some exotic species, such as polar bear, tiger or elephant. It proved that you were wealthy enough to be able to travel to exotic climes for the purpose of sport. It was, in short, an alpha male activity –

exemplified by Hemingway and Denys Finch Hatton, one of whose clients in 1928 and 1930 was the Prince of Wales, later the Duke of Windsor.

Despite hunting being considered a gentlemanly sport, whether grouse and pheasant, trout and pike, or lion and tiger, it had its detractors. The Victorian dramatist, W. S. Gilbert, observed: "Deer-stalking would be a very fine sport if only the deer had guns." Hunting today is a rich man's game – it was ever thus and although books, such as *Practical Taxidermy*, by Montagu Browne, published in 1884, did devote considerable space to "Decoying and Trapping Animals", few taxidermists were, or indeed are, hunters. Most modern taxidermists and artists are anxious to emphasise

LEFT Big game trophies are littered around a mid-twentieth century fireplace in an over-the-top display that is very much of its era.

that their specimens died of natural causes and not in the name of taxidermy. Today there are legal controls in place that govern good practice; taxidermists that mount trophies must ensure that specimens were caught and killed in line with legislation and must have the paperwork to prove it.

With the benefit of hindsight we can see the damage that unregulated hunting wrought. Game hunters themselves were quick to notice the effects; William Adolph Baillie-Grohman produced numerous tomes describing his hunting expeditions in detail. In *Sport and Life in the Hunting Grounds of Western America and British Colombia* he notes: "in those days one had no idea that the extermination of big game would take place with such appalling rapidity. Tens of thousands were butchered for the sake of a few shillings obtained for the skin." Baillie-Grohman also acknowledges that the destruction of the bulk of big game in the United States was the work of one single generation, which he notes was an unpleasant truth for the "Makers of the West".

Nevertheless, hunters and collectors, whether through passion for their sport or a reluctance to face the truth, had mixed feelings about the enactment of legislation. Baillie-Grohman observes: "If you had told the average American twenty years ago that before the century would end the enact-

ment of game laws – not the mere passing but also their enforcement – would become a burning question from the Atlantic to the Pacific, you would have been informed that you knew nothing about "the greatest and freest people on earth".

PREVIOUS PAGE The taking of fox heads, tail and pads as trophies was a common hunting practice until the mid-nineteenth century. Fox-hunting was banned in Scotland in 2002 and in England and Wales in 2005, but taxidermists have a ready supply as so many foxes die in traffic accidents.

ABOVE The hunter William Adolph Baillie Grohman (1851–1921) celebrated the glories of hunting in his books, but also bore witness to, and railed against, the terrible destruction of big game in the USA.

ABOVE This grisly photograph of a pile of poached rhino heads was taken by taxidermist Rowland Ward and first published in 1876. The illegal continuing trade in rhino horns means that poaching is still a major threat to the survival of the species.

OVERLEAF Trans-African Taxidermists in South Africa have specialised in hunting trophies since 1951. All post-1947 hunting trophies must be accompanied by appropriate paperwork that complies with international trade legislation.

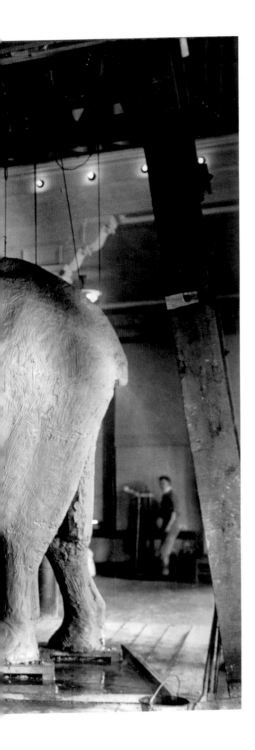

Major Percy Powell-Cotton notes in his book, *In Unknown Africa*:

> The protection of game is doubtless a wise and necessary precaution, but it might, I think, be attempted in a more practical spirit. Under the present system the Reserves are vast areas over which no sort of control is exercised, and where, in consequence, the indigenous inhabitants can slaughter at their own sweet will, while armed bands of traders constantly pass through them, and kill without discrimination for meat and hide. The … sportsman, if he be so minded … can equally well shoot to his heart's content, provided he throws away the trophies. One day, when it is too late, it will be found that a species belonging to some special district has been extinguished, and it will then be realised that the only specimens extant are in some museum on the Continent.

If hunting is to be judged, it is interesting that the collectors drew clear distinctions between their kills and those of the sportsman: "It is a deplorable fact that the authorities have shown themselves unable to distinguish between a man who carefully preserves the entire skin and the skull of nearly every animal he kills, and one who merely shoots

LEFT American taxidermist Carl Akeley works on an elephant in 1914 as part of his planned group, *The Alarm*, for the African Hall at the American Museum of Natural History.

for the sake of killing or for securing the longest horn," observes Powell-Cotton.

Baillie-Grohman, however, defends the sport: "My chief aim in visiting the Rockies was to bag big heads. To get a dozen wapiti antlers over 60 in [152 cm] in length, or a like number of bighorn with a circumference of 17 in [43 cm] and 18 in [45.5 cm], meant the securing of prizes which only a few sportsmen who have visited the Rockies have been able to obtain. And while I will not deny that, notwithstanding great care and discrimination in the selection of one's quarry, one now and again killed animals which, when they lay dead on the ground before one, turned out to be smaller than one thought, and whose trophies therefore would not warrant transportation; these were the occurrences one tried to avoid as much as possible." Baillie-Grohman was clearly interested in acquiring the biggest and best specimens he could and notes that: "the largest of the great number [of deer] I have killed had twenty-six tines, but I believe Mr Theodore Roosevelt has one bearing the extraordinary number of thirty-nine."

He also describes his experience with Bighorn: "The horns of the largest bighorn are of stupendous girth, the head weighing as much as 40 lb [18 kg]. I was fortunate enough to bag, among the

RIGHT Workers shave animal skins at a taxidermists' firm at Mysore, India in 1929. In its heyday the Van Ingen & Van Ingen workshops employed some 150 staff and processed around 400 tigers per year.

seventy or eighty bighorn I got, an uncommonly fine ram, each of his horns girthing 19 in [48 cm] at the base. It is – or rather was – for I lost this grand trophy by fire – probably one of the finest heads of which we have any record." In the same chapter he notes, without apparent irony: "Man has exterminated many species of wild game in his day, but at no period of history has he succeeded in destroying animals with the appalling rapidity observable today." He adds that: "in the 1880s frontiersmen engaged in hide hunting, received a mere 50 cents for each of the many thousands of bison skins they took. Fifteen years later bison were practically extinct."

Whatever one's view on hunting, Baillie-Grohman's account makes for riveting reading, it is a *Boy's Own* adventure laid bare. He highlights a problem that besets all hunters and collectors: "Transporting these big heads was the chief difficulty in my case, as only a few horses were available for that duty. Transporting wapiti [elk] antlers on pack-horses, often for weeks at a time, is a most troublesome job, not only because one cannot get more than two heads on one horse, but on account of their bulk, which makes travel through timbered country most difficult, if not entirely impossible."

It is perhaps the logistics that are most impressive. Mary Jobe Akeley, describes the work involved in skinning a giraffe in her book *Carl Akeley's Africa*:

… it was ten o' clock; the weldt was already shimmering in blazing heat and the hottest hours of the day were still to come. It was a herculean task. The tarpaulin was thrown up as a sun-canopy protecting the giraffe. Carl and Rockwell had been skinning for an hour, but the amount of work accomplished seemed only to increase the size of the giant. … As soon as a square foot was removed, salt was rubbed on both sides for the extraction of the water. Other porters, as soon as the muscles were exposed, removed the flesh. … After eleven hours in the field and six hours of grilling, back-breaking preparatory work, the specimen was loaded into the truck at four o' clock and taken into camp for the completion of the skinning of the hoofs and horns and for the re-salting of the skin … All the following day the work continued. At last the giraffe skeleton was clean and hoisted high in a big acacia tree out of the reach of marauding hyenas; and that night we all gathered silently around the work-fly where, by the light of half a dozen lanterns, Carl and Rockwell and Raddatz were still doing yeoman service in making the big giraffe skin into the nearest possible approach to a piece of velvet …

LEFT A tiger head by Van Ingen & Van Ingen from 1935 resides peacefully next to a superb example of Victorian taxidermy, a dome of tropical South American birds circa 1860.

OVERLEAF An American hunter poses proudly with his collection of trophies circa 1915. Being a good shot was an essential skill in rural communities.

ABOVE Artist Angela Singer recycles old hunting trophies in her contemporary artwork. Here "Nepenthe I", 2011 – taxidermy pheasant and mixed media.

RIGHT "Chilled Lamb 04" by Angela Singer, 2004, recycled taxidermy, painted blowflies and jewels.

Despite no trace of squeamishness in her account, Mary Jobe Akeley did not enjoy shooting. After she bagged her first lion she turned to her husband and said: "Thank you Carl, but I don't think I'll be doing any more hunting."

In both India and Africa taxidermy businesses sprang up to meet the demands of the big-game hunter. Van Ingen & Van Ingen of Mysore, South India, founded in the 1890s, specialised in hunting trophies and, in its heyday, employed an astounding 150 staff. The company prospered until the 1970s, when big game hunting was banned in India and Kenya, and managed to stagger on for another twenty years until its closure in 1999. Taxidermist, Rowland Ward, produced a *Sportsman's Handbook*, advising huntershow best to preserve specimens in the field. Ward also wrote, *Records of Big Game*, which ran to many editions, detailing all the record breaking specimens of various species and that doubtless fired hunters on to greater competitive endeavours. Baillie-Grohman describes the "superb trophies" on show at The American Trophy Exhibition, held at Earl's Court in 1887: "It was a loan collection the like of which the present generation will probably not see again, for only those who took upon themselves the endless trouble and responsibility of inducing owners of choice trophies to dismantle their walls of their treasures, can form an idea of the hard work and the immense amount of correspondence it entailed upon those involved who initiated the movement."

Hunting trophies continued to be popular long after domestic taxidermy lost its allure. Trophies epitomise the prowess of alpha males; commissioned by royalty, they featured in Hollywood film sets and spoke of the drama and romance of a bygone era – indeed they feature in period costume drama today. And trophies are still commissioned and remain hugely popular in both Russia and the United States.

Angela Singer, a keen animal rights activist, recycles old hunting trophies in her contemporary artwork, as she says: "to honour the animal's life". In the magazine, *Antennae*, Singer observes: "I think some people fear the physicality of art that uses taxidermy. Taxidermy shrinks the animal and botching taxidermy gives the animal back its presence, making it too big to ignore." The artist had a museum diorama donated to her of a full size trophy kill that she is using for her confrontational work.

LEFT An example of the extraordinary quality of contemporary taxidermy of a red deer by Dutch taxidermist Maurice Bouten, who is a World Taxidermy Championship award winner.

CHAPTER FOUR

realism

"They are the proof that something was there and no longer is. Like a stain. And the stillness of them is boggling."

DIANE ARBUS (PHOTOGRAPHER)

The National Museum of Scotland, which recently overhauled its taxidermy display, wanted to enable visitors to see animals in apparently typical behaviour, here a flock of geese fly through the upper gallery.

If the aim of taxidermy is to create as life-like a specimen as possible then many pieces leave much to be desired. The art of representational taxidermy takes years to learn, it combines a taxidermist's skill with an artist's eye and a sculptor's vision. It also relies on having a sound anatomical knowledge of one's specimen. This goes some way to explaining why many of the creatures featured in the old masters were not truly representational. Artists such as Rembrandt and Dürer utilised taxidermy as reference material, but if the taxidermist's specimen was anatomically incorrect then the caricature was perpetuated.

Much early taxidermy is so far from being representational that it has the ghoulish effect of a circus sideshow. And while the work of Victorian taxidermists became more figurative, its essential style is romantic; butterflies and beetles mounted to produce a shimmering iridescent mosaic, birds and animals placed in saccharine, or high-drama scenes that, no matter how beautifully executed, have the fantasy feel of a miniature filmset.

With a wealth of reference material at their fingertips the modern taxidermist has no excuse not to produce accurate models, but even then they face dilemmas, as taxidermist Carl Church explains: "You have to ask yourself, do you want perfection or do you want life? The best taxidermy I have seen shows the bird looking very much alive, maybe with a few feathers sticking out", he explains, "but when you compete in America they want perfection, with all the feather tracks properly laid."

Church, who is so skilled that he has claimed prizes at the notoriously picky World Taxidermy Championship, says that one of the keys to success is to study live animals: "Good reference material is important; you need to know how birds stand and how their feathers lie. If an eagle has a fluffed out head it has it for a reason – you have to get the entire bird in the right mood. It is the same as drawing someone in a relaxed pose, with a tense look on their face – it doesn't look right."

Specialising in bird taxidermy, Church is constantly striving to perfect his technique: "I try to produce an accurate manikin. I struggled with the bind-up method for years [see pages 150–3], but it didn't work for me." He learned that in Europe many taxidermists carve their bodies, or manikins, out of wood: "It is important to produce an accurate body, which is structurally sound – to get good foundations, and then I can put the bird in any position." For a man who is so interested in the significance of reference material and anatomical exactitude, Church is dedicated to recreating the long-extinct Dodo.

RIGHT An award winning, exclusive cased work by Carl Church, from 2008, featuring two Icelandic puffins.

If realism is the goal then everyone agrees that it is more difficult for commercial taxidermists to achieve; perfection takes long hours of work. Customers do not always understand that technical excellence comes at a price and, while you may be able to purchase a specimen more cheaply, quality will be compromised; you get what you pay for. Museum taxidermists tend to spend longer on their mounts, as technical excellence is a prerequisite and they are not limited by commercial constraints. The Museum of Scotland, which has the only working taxidermy department in the country, recently overhauled its galleries to public acclaim. Andrew Kitchener, Principal Curator of Vertebrate Biology, explains: "The role of taxidermy is to help us to understand the natural world. To show animals exhibiting behaviour that would be difficult to see in the wild and to explain how animals adapted to their particular lifestyle." He sees the museum's function as being "inspirational" and points out that: "It's about trying to capture the imagination and to make visitors believe that in the next moment that animal is going to move. In that way you can create awe, interest and fascination."

Kitchener and his team have been engaged in the most ambitious taxidermy project in the UK for a generation and the amount of new work is

unprecedented. The department started working on the exhibits five years ago, some of the largest pieces, such as the giraffe and the rhinoceros had to be outsourced to a Dutch firm, Bouten and Son, as the department had neither the time or the space to undertake everything themselves.

LEFT This detail from a work by Carl Church, from 2010, was inspired by an Archibald Thorburn painting of "The Lost Stag". The female golden eagle, an old lady well into her twenties, had spent her life at a bird of prey centre.

ABOVE An exclusive work featuring a male Eider Duck by Carl Church, from 2010. The mature adult bird was captive bred and had been part of a privately owned water fowl collection before his death.

Significantly, they had the raw material. "We collected a lot of stuff in anticipation of there being a major exhibition", Kitchener explains, although he emphasises that in the case of rare or extinct specimens they obviously make do with what they already have.

An aye-aye (lemur) specimen that demonstrates a remarkable feeding adaptation – an extremely long, slender and dexterous middle finger that allows it to extract insects from tiny holes in trees – highlights the quest for realism. "It was a very difficult specimen to get hold of and we could only source a visual reference for the head. For months the carcass was set up and we kept playing around with it but it just wasn't right," comments Kitchener, who eventually acquired images via a director at London Zoo to overcome the problems. He adds: "it is as authentic as it can be and it was a real challenge, but it is a beautiful piece."

Modern museum collections will only utilise specimens that have died of natural causes, most have had long lives and met their end naturally in zoos and wildlife parks across the world. Indeed Kitchener and colleagues confess that space can be an issue: "People can be quite determined that we take an animal and preserve it, especially when it is an old favourite. They don't want to incinerate it; they want it to live on, to continue

ABOVE RIGHT The National Museum of Scotland commissioned Dutch firm Bouten to make the giraffe, seen here prior to shipping, as the Museum could not produce all the work required in-house.

RIGHT The Bouten giraffe in situ in The Museum of Scotland. Visitors can view it from ground level and go to the upper galleries to look down on its impressive, straining reach.

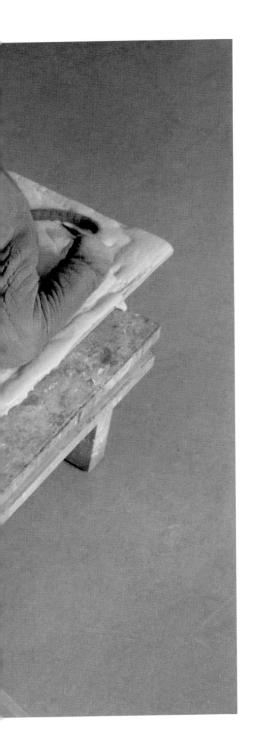

to be useful. When we started we had to do a lot of work to persuade people that what we were doing was okay and it took a while. But it is becoming commonplace now. If you are interested in taxidermy it is a tremendous waste to just dispose of the animal when it can go on being beautiful."

Phil Howard, taxidermist at the Museum of Scotland highlights that it is rare for a specimen to come in and only be used for taxidermy: "Part of the reason that we prepare fibreglass manikins is so that we can recover the skeleton for research collections. We take a muscle sample for DNA, the specimen will have multiple roles within the organisation and this is why it is easy for us to get specimens from zoos and wildlife parks, because they live on in their usefulness." Dolly the sheep, the first mammal to be cloned, is one such specimen, she sadly only lived to be six years of age but her celebrity status continues and she draws large crowds. Her taxidermy form even travelled to Hungary for the opening of a new science museum in Budapest.

Another groundbreaking exhibit was that of a baby elephant, which utilised the technique of erosion casting. This process, a science and an art, involves putting an animal corpse into its desired position, coating it with silicone rubber to create a mould and then leaving the body to decompose.

LEFT This baby elephant was stillborn and taxidermist Phil Howard worked with sculptor and taxidermist Emily Mayer to produce an erosion cast that is impossibly vulnerable and life-like.

"Zoos and wildlife parks often want their treasured animals to be taken for taxidermy when they die."

When the decomposition process is underway and the skin starts to slip – a few days in the case of a small mammal, but considerably longer the larger the specimen – the carcass can be removed leaving a rubber shell. Creating the resin cast is a painstaking process that reflects minute changes in skin colour and freckles to produce a precise impression of the skin and preserve every wrinkle and hair. The end result is, near as damn it, an exact replica of the animal.

Howard worked on the baby elephant exhibit with sculptor and taxidermist Emily Mayer and admits that the scale of the project was challenging. "The problem with erosion casting is that you invest so much in the process, but if any little thing goes wrong with it the specimen is ruined. A safari park offered us a stillborn baby elephant, we didn't need it because we already had one, but they were insistent that we take it, they even delivered it to our door. As we had a spare it was an ideal opportunity to try out the technique." The resulting specimen, a new-born struggling to rise, has a heart-breaking vulnerability, but Howard is quick to emphasise the limitations of erosion casting: "What you are doing is replicating a dead animal and it is hard to get that dynamism, to get it looking alive and modern taxidermy should be engaging and dynamic."

RIGHT The work of Mike Gadd, an award winning taxidermist, exemplifies the extraordinary standards achieved by contemporary taxidermists, here an impossibly life-like grey squirrel.

OVERLEAF Museums used to employ taxidermists as a matter of course; here taxidermy students receive tuition in animal anatomy from model-maker Arthur Hayward in the basement of the Natural History Museum, 1968.

Contemporary taxidermy presents great demands on its exponents and poses have to be aesthetically pleasing as well as scientifically accurate. As Kitchener observes: "it has to convey the message that we want to send in terms of animal behaviour. If you freeze-frame an animal running there are phases when it looks daft and if a mount doesn't quite work you have to realise where it went wrong and start again." The attention to detail extends to the groundwork – the leaves and grasses that give an extra layer of authenticity. Phil Howard explains: "The New Caledonian Crow uses a twig to get larvae out of rotten wood. We could have used any old twig, but the one that we have was actually fashioned by a New Caledonian Crow in New Caledonia. It is absolutely authentic and is a registered specimen within the museum."

The Museum of Scotland deserves to be saluted for promoting the value of taxidermy and recognising its appeal to a contemporary audience; the new galleries have been consistently popular with the public. Nevertheless, not all museums have been so far-sighted. The wholesale destruction of so much museum taxidermy is little short of a tragedy. As collector Errol Fuller observes: "Over the last sixty years natural history departments in museums have allowed themselves to be trampled by events and popular thinking. They haven't lobbied for grants and funding as other departments have." Fuller is appalled by what he views as the hypocrisy of people who pretend, or imagine, they despise all taxidermy in the name of sensitivity and decency: "I have no objection to someone not liking it or not wanting it in their house, but they haven't appreciated that taxidermy has its place in history with as much value as, for instance, a piece of early porcelain."

In 1999, the Smithsonian Institution in the United States broke up many of its historic dioramas in a re-building process, the excuse was that the dioramas formed part of the fabric of the building and were, therefore, impossible to conserve. But other exhibits were also lost, including an eighty-nine foot blue whale, first constructed in 1956 and which briefly appeared for sale on eBay, although in the end it was broken up as it was too big to be removed as a whole.

Representational taxidermy also has a place in the commercial world. Victorian and Edwardian photographers recognised its allure and utilised stuffed herons to pose with babies and small children, while early glamour models in a state of dishabille snuggled up to lions, tigers and bears for dramatic effect. Seaside photographers were still using taxidermy as late as the 1950s, with day-trippers perching improbably on stuffed lions.

LEFT A thrush by wildlife artist David Leggett, 2012. Leggett's taxidermy work is clean and simple, and is designed to allow the beauty of the creature to be displayed without artifice.

OVERLEAF An uncased baby tapir of unknown origin. The tapir is nocturnal; its diet consists of fruits, berries and leaves. Adult tapirs can reach 2m (7ft) in length, 1m (3ft) in height and weigh between 150–300kg (330–700lb).

Advertisers also utilise the commercial value of animals. Simon Wilson, founder of Animatronic Animals, who supplies taxidermy for film and television drama as well as commercials, explains: "Filming is expensive and directors need to be able to guarantee results, a taxidermy animal doesn't act up. I am often asked to produce an animal that looks as though it has died. In the past, they would have drugged a live animal to get the desired effect, but they can't do that anymore and that is where we come in."

Wilson has supplied robins for advertisements for Ribena (juice drink) and Lockets (lozengers), and a song thrush for Heineken beer. He has

ABOVE This taxidermy chick, with a rubber cockerel's comb, was made by Simon Wilson of Animatronic Animals, in 1992, for a French billboard advertisement.

RIGHT A fully animatronic creation covered in penguin feathers made by Simon Wilson of Animatronic Animals for a German film, *Amundsen der Pinguin*.

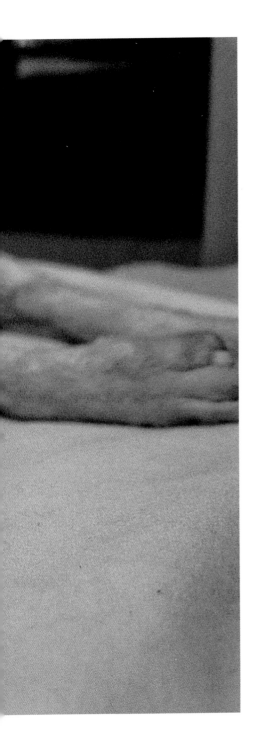

contributed to films such as *Harry Potter*, *The Secret Garden*, *Charlie and the Chocolate Factory* and *Casino Royale* as well as natural history programmes. His work is fast-paced and a world away from the tightly crafted perfection demanded by museums, but Wilson's realism is about the final effect – he thinks nothing of transforming a female lion into a tiger with the use of hair-dye and skins are used repeatedly, dismantled and kept flexible for the next project.

Emily Mayer, sculptor and taxidermist, equates the realism produced in modern taxidermy by the best practitioners to wildlife art: "it's a very niche art, an area that is more like illustration than anything else." Whatever else it does, the new realism in taxidermy is a wonderful educational tool, as Dr Pat Morris, former Senior Lecturer in zoology and taxidermy enthusiast observes: "When I was a kid living in the East End of London the only wildlife was in museums."

LEFT "Bertie" by Emily Mayer, resin, hair and whiskers, 2011. Bertie is a fox-hound from a hunt kennel, donated when he met his end after a long life. Emily produced this work for herself and Bertie is a permanent fixture in her life.

OVERLEAF Swiss taxidermist Matthias Fahrni specialises in working with very small fish. This spirlin won him the Best in World title at the 2003 World Taxidermy Championships. To give some idea of the scale of his work this spirlin measures just 10cm (4in) in length.

cutting edge

"The life of the dead is placed in the memory of the living."

MARCUS TULLIUS CICERO (PHILOSOPHER)

The Critics by Emily Mayer, 2005: wood, steel, leather, copper, epoxy resin and lamp. The piece, a tongue-in-cheek critique of her own work, combined Mayer's found sculpture and erosion cast taxidermy for the first time and was exhibited at The World Taxidermy Championships, 2005.

If taxidermy was out of fashion for the second half of the twentieth century it has achieved a dramatic turnaround in the first decade of the new millennium. The runaway success in 1991 of Damien Hirst's shark in formaldehyde, *The Physical Impossibility of Death in the Mind of Someone Living*, and the following works, *Mother and Child (Divided)* 1993 and *Away from the Flock*, 1994, while not taxidermy, seemed to mark a shift in public consciousness. Certainly most taxidermists will cite Hirst's work as influential in as much as it does not shrink away from death, but embraces it. The lawyer and academic, Anthony Julius, calls it "taboo-breaking art".

Art that utilises taxidermy has become achingly fashionable. Its list of influential A-List punters appears to have kick-started a resurgence of aesthetic interest in not only antique, but also contemporary taxidermy. The stigma that was attached to owning taxidermy has gone – along with a new understanding that contemporary taxidermy is distinctly green, as artist and taxidermist Polly Morgan says: "It's a form of recycling as far as I can see. When people criticise me I always say that the worst thing I am doing is depriving a crow of its meal. I don't buy into the argument that it is disrespectful to the animal. Animals don't mourn their dead, they generally eat

RIGHT *Black Sheep*, 2007: glass, painted stainless steel, silicone, acrylic, plastic, sheep and formaldehyde solution (1091 x 1623 x 641mm). The challenging nature of Damien Hirst's ground-breaking work, though not taxidermy, is widely credited with kick-starting interest in the subject.

them." And perhaps the renewed enthusiasm for the subject comes from the public understanding that, as the disclaimer always puts it, no animals were harmed in this process.

Polly Morgan owns that doing her own taxidermy work is very much part of the creative process: "I would never claim to be one of the best taxidermists technically, but to me, making it myself is important because the work that I have in mind when I start, is quite often different to the work that I end up with. I make decisions along the way and if I had someone else making it for me then those decisions wouldn't be made."

Both Morgan, and sculptor and taxidermist Emily Mayer, note the distinction between their contemporary art and traditional taxidermy – principally that it makes no pretence to being anything other than a dead thing. As Mayer explains: "By portraying an animal as dead you get much closer to the truth and it is more disturbing. I am not interested in making pieces of work where people aren't challenged. The total has to be more than the sum of its parts; otherwise it is just an effigy."

Morgan, whose website emphatically states that she only works with animals that are road casualties or who have been donated by pet owners or vets after natural or unpreventable deaths, never

ABOVE *Receiver* by Polly Morgan, 2009: taxidermy quail chicks and Bakelite handset. The work, influenced by pop artists and surrealists, juxtaposes and contrasts textures and visualises sound coming out of the receiver.

RIGHT *Systemic Inflammation* by Polly Morgan, 2010, is named after a condition that can kill. It features taxidermy finches and canaries, some dyed orange, flying above a scorched cage, redolent of a phoenix rising from the ashes.

"The scale and settings are often unnatural but the animals are never anthropomorphised."

POLLY MORGAN

---

wanted to do traditional taxidermy: "I thought I could bring something new to it. Because so many taxidermists mimic the natural habitat of the animal and it suddenly struck me around the time of my first lesson that there were so few different settings and I couldn't work out why that was. Obviously there were a few contemporary artists who used taxidermy in their artwork, but it was more of a one-off thing."

Morgan says she was always fascinated by taxidermy and describes a pivotal moment in her career when she realised that the only way she could obtain animals in the settings she wanted was to either commission a taxidermist or under-

take the work herself. She explains that: "Birds have such a good posture when they die – on their backs with their head on one side. It creates a heart-shape, their wings are open and I find something quite touching about how they look – peaceful but vulnerable at the same time."

If you speak to any taxidermist their formative influences are hugely significant. Most of them, like Morgan and Mayer have a dormant interest, they collected shells or skulls, they watched birds in the garden, pressed flowers, or spent hours in museums with their noses pressed against glass cases of taxidermy. Mayer was drawn to the exhibits preserved in formaldehyde at the Horniman

LEFT A detail from *Archipelago*, by Polly Morgan, 2012, which deals with the relationship between parasites and hosts. The mushrooms are cast in rubber and the pig is cast in silicone with a taxidermy finch on the shoulder. The work is from the exhibition "Endless Plains", which is a translation of Serengeti, and describes cycles of life and death, representing nature in an unrealistic way.

Museum, London (see pages 48–51): "they don't have any of that stuff on show now", she observes.

All appear to be animal lovers nurturing injured birds back to health and rescuing un-wanted cats and dogs. That being said they do not fear the harsh reality of their work, as Morgan says: "As soon as I started skinning birds my interest flourished, the work satisfied both my scientific and artistic sides, part butchery, part sculpture I always call it."

Morgan admits that she was hooked from the start: "I was so excited to have these creatures in my freezer that I hadn't worked on before, and this alone would start me off. I would defrost something and start playing around with it, putting it on things and in things and trying to work out how I liked it. I see it as a beautiful raw material to work with." The juxtaposition of different materials is important to her: "I like smooth shiny clear surfaces next to very dense feathers. To begin with it was an instinctive thing, putting different elements together. Once I'd got over the initial thrill of doing taxidermy I started thinking more deeply about the work before I embarked on it."

Her distinctive work immediately attracted the attention of the artistic glitterati. *Still Life After Death* shows a white rabbit curled on top of a magician's hat, and *To Every Seed His Own Body* features a small blue-tit, eyes closed as if dead, on a prayer book inside a glass dome. *Receiver* (see page 126) utilises an old-fashioned telephone receiver in which quail chick heads, mouths gaping, in a silent shriek, crowd the earpiece. Then there is the gargantuan sculptural piece *Departures*, which is based on a Victorian flying machine apparently

drawn by pigeons, starlings, canaries and three huge white-backed vultures.

Morgan's latest works are on a grand scale and she says that she has moved more towards abstraction, in work inspired by corpses in various stages of decay that she saw littering the Serengeti (see page 128): "They looked really beautiful, as though the animal had just fallen and been hollowed out by vultures, which is pretty much what happens."

The sculptor and taxidermist, Emily Mayer, started doing taxidermy when she was twelve years old, she learned from a book by Leon L. Pray, a typically impenetrable taxidermy "how-to" book. Her first specimen was a dead baby rabbit that her father brought home for her to work on and which she retains to this day. For a first piece it is astonishingly good and is perhaps indicative of her raw talent. She must also have startled her primary school teacher with a project on local wildlife that featured a moleskin which she had dried herself.

Mayer is a perfectionist, both her sculpture and her taxidermy utilise found materials and she constantly experiments with new techniques. Her curiosity was aroused by an erosion cast piglet by Derek Frampton that she saw in 1983 and she started experimenting with the technique:

RIGHT A detail from *Harbour* by Polly Morgan, 2012, featuring a taxidermy fox with a silicone rubber octopus bursting from within it and throttling in it, and in turn being "pollinated" by wrens. The work illustrates the cycle of host and parasite and is symbolic of new life and germination.

ABOVE *Final Voyage – Precious Cargo* by Emily Mayer, 2006: epoxy resin, hair, suitcase. The piece, which features an erosion cast Yorkshire terrier, alludes to people who love their dogs perhaps too much. It is inspired by Mayer being brought a dead dog in a suitcase to work on and by reports of people trying to smuggle dogs through customs in a suitcase and accidentally asphyxiating them.

ABOVE *Sweetmeats # – Sugar Mice 1* by Emily Mayer, 2007, printed cardboard, resin, hair and whiskers. The work, featuring erosion cast mice, is a humorous take on the strange notion of people feeding their children sugar mice.

"Basically the whole body is covered in rubber, then you rot the insides out – that is the basics. You end up with a rubber mould with nothing but the hair trapped in it. On the insides of the mould are the roots of the hair, which were in the skin. The interior is then cast in resin so that it picks up the roots of the hair and finally you destroy the rubber coating. What you are left with, what looks like skin, is actually resin. The taxidermy I do now is almost all about the surface, I mean there is nothing left inside, I am just making a carbon copy of what I have got. Whereas the sculptures are about the mechanics of movement. I understand that because I have studied the animals so carefully and taken them apart – you get a sense of the movement."

Erosion casting, or skin replacement taxidermy, is not a speedy process, the time it takes is variable, rats decompose in a matter of days, but some animals can take months. Mayer maintains that the technique is not the modern version of taxidermy, just another way of doing specific things. "It works very well with certain animals in certain

PREVIOUS PAGE *The Dog's Bollocks* by Emily Mayer, 2002, glass, ceramic, plastic epoxy resin, hair, specimens in spirit. This work was designed to prove that erosion casting was taxidermy, it took Mayer a long time to find a rat in good enough condition to work on. The piece took a mass of awards at The Guild of Taxidermists Awards, 2005.

RIGHT Hyperrealist imagery from the Italian artist Maurizio Cattelan, whose work often includes disturbing taxidermy images. Here *Untitled*, 1997, features an ostrich with its head apparently buried in the floor.

positions," she elaborates, "erosion casting gives an exact reproduction."

Mayer is not interested in animated taxidermy: "I can appreciate it and the amazing work that goes into it. When people really get it right you think – wow. But I prefer the more contemplative work; the concept that at any moment the animal might move, that if you turn away and turn back it might just have shifted slightly. There is a presence about that work that the high action stuff doesn't have." Hence the reason perhaps that much of her work features animals that are sleeping or dead. Her studio floor is home to a number of large, apparently sleeping dogs, Bertie the Foxhound (see page 118) and Rosie the Collie – all erosion cast work.

Mayer's taxidermy, though disturbingly real, is often playful. For instance, she made a piglet handbag for a bad-taste party, and a startlingly life-like rat rolling a jar containing a pair of canine testicles – entitled *The Dog's Bollocks* (see pages 134–5). The contents of the jar came from a neighbour's dog that had to be neutered. In another piece, *Final Voyage* (see page 132), she depicts a small dog curled up in a suitcase – a reflection of how one specimen arrived at her studio. Mayer explains: "I get quite offended by some taxidermy because it is done so badly.

LEFT *La Ballata di Trotsky* by Maurizio Cattelan, 1999, taxidermied horse, leather saddlery, rope and pulley. The horse featured was a racehorse called Tiramisu given to the artist after it died of natural causes. The legs were extended. Seen here as part of a Cattelan retrospective at the Guggenheim in New York, 2011.

LEFT *Bidibidobidiboo* by Maurizio Cattelan, 1996: taxidermied squirrel, ceramic, Formica, wood, paint and steel, 45 x 60 x 58cm. An anthropomorphic scene depicting a squirrel that has committed suicide.

ABOVE *A Fragile Happiness* by Chlöe Brown, 2002, features a stag's head, birds and glass. The piece depicts a comic tragedy, the stag weeps because he is dead and because the birds mistake his antlers for branches.

If anyone who is messing around with dead things can't do it properly it is an insult to the animal."

Both Morgan and Mayer are unusual in that they undertake all the taxidermy work themselves, but an increasing number of contemporary artists utilise taxidermy in their work. The Italian artist Maurizio Cattelan is famous for sculptures such as *The Ballad of Trotsky* (see pages 138–9) – a horse suspended from a ceiling which sold for £1.15 million – or *Bidibidobidiboo* (see page 140), which shows a squirrel that has committed suicide in a kitchen. Scottish artist, David Shrigley, uses

ABOVE *Things Will Never Be The Same Again* by Chlöe Brown, 2001, features taxidermy animals and birds, artificial snow, snow machine and flood light – a tableau of birds and animals frozen in time.

RIGHT A detail from *Things Will Never Be The Same Again* by Chlöe Brown. All three rabbits are weeping, while other creatures watch intently, caught in a snow globe fantasy.

taxidermy to animate his own deadpan jokes; for example, a Jack Russell standing upright and holding a placard that reads *I'm Dead*, or *Nutless* – a headless squirrel holding its head in its hands.

Even the fashion industry has embraced taxidermy; designer Gareth Pugh and milliner Philip Treacy have both used taxidermy birds on hats. The singer, Lady Gaga, has stepped out in white dove shoes by Iris Schieferstein, who makes a point of combining fashion and taxidermy. The late Alexander McQueen worked with Simon Wilson of Animatronic Animals utilising antlers, heron and flamingo wings, feathers, horsehair and entire taxidermy creatures in numerous collections.

As taxidermy trainer, David Leggett, observes: "when people asked me what I did I used to say that I was a wildlife sculptor. If you told them what you actually did they looked askance – taxidermists were viewed as evil people in bloody aprons who went out and killed things, but attitudes have changed. I maintain that you can teach anyone the basic process – skinning, fleshing-out and dressing the bird. The art is in the setting up, that is when the magic happens."

RIGHT Artist David Shrigley's taxidermied Jack Russell holds up a darkly ironic placard proclaiming *I'm Dead* in his his Brain Activity exhibition at London's Hayward Gallery, 2012.

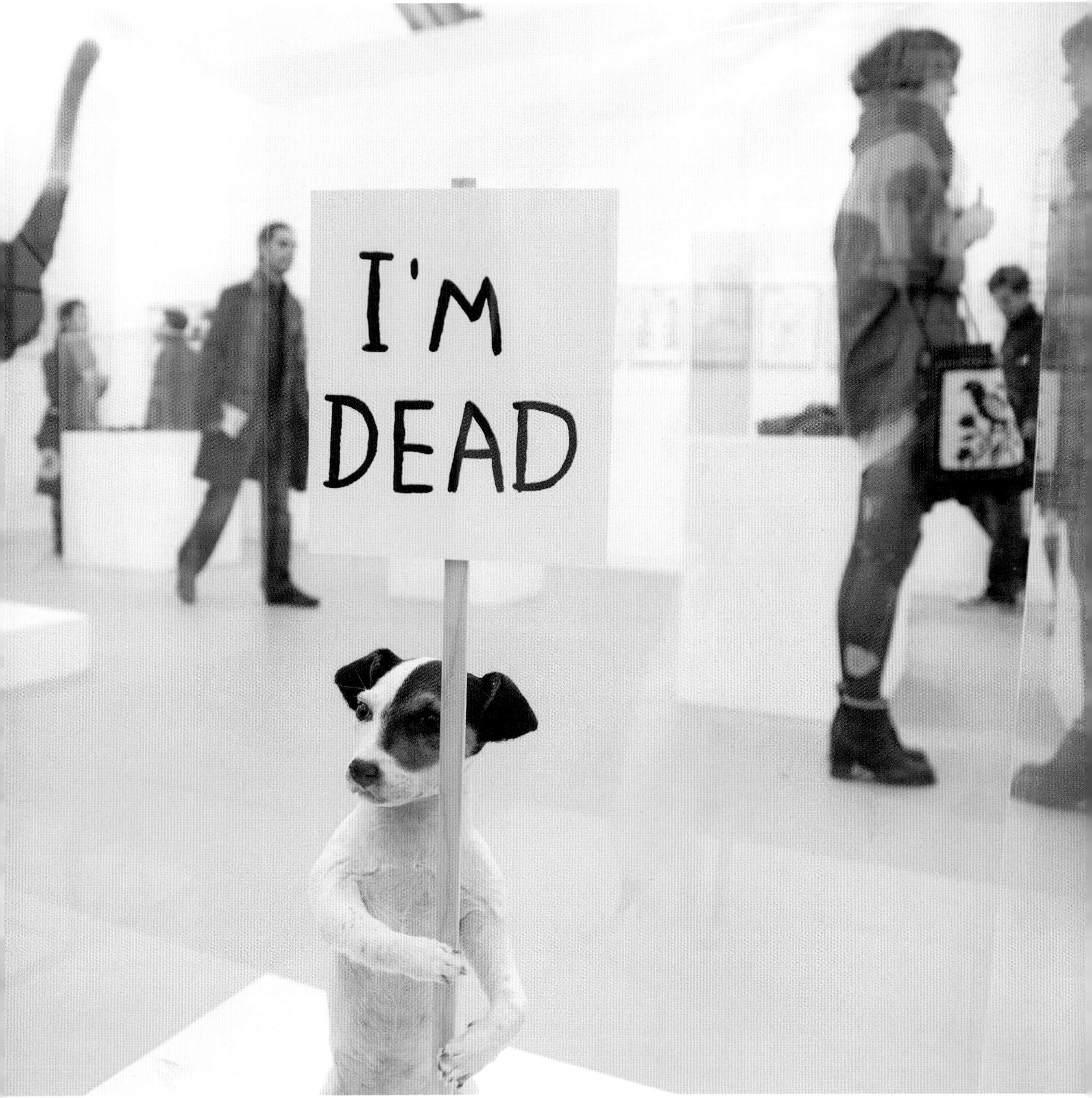
I'M
DEAD

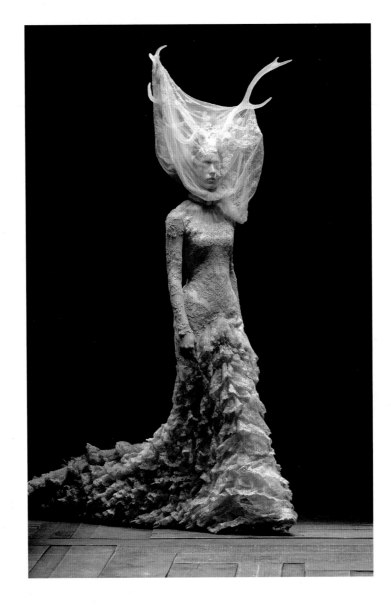

ABOVE Alexander McQueen sends out a white ruffled antler-wearing bride in his Autumn/Winter 2006 collection, dedicated to his friend and exotic millinery enthusiast Isabella Blow.

RIGHT Alexander McQueen at his gothic and theatrical best with this fantastical piece of millinery from his Spring/Summer 2001 collection.

the craft of taxidermy

"Any relic of the dead is precious, if they were valued living."

EMILY BRONTË (AUTHOR)

A group of uncased taxidermy, from left to right:
a Parameles, a koala bear, a horned grebe from
the Julius Brenchley Collection, once exhibited in
Maidstone museum and an Echidna, or spiny anteater.

The raw material of taxidermy is a skin. Arguably anything with a skin can be utilised – including humans; though the latter, the stuff of horror movies made flesh and immortalised by Norman Bates in *Psycho*, is blessedly rare. Those who are squeamish should perhaps remind themselves that all skins go through a form of this basic process, from today's politically incorrect fur coats, to the everyday leather and suede items that we take for granted, such as shoes, handbags, belts, purses, wallets and even furniture upholstery. All are skins that have been cleaned and worked to produce a particular effect. A taxidermy skin is no different.

A taxidermist needs a fresh specimen to work on; bodies decompose at different rates depending on the temperature and the weather conditions, but if decomposition has progressed too far the skin will be useless. The work of the modern-day stuffer has been made considerably easier since the invention of the freezer, which preserves bodies until required; prior to this the taxidermist had to work very fast indeed.

The basic process is the same, although the technique varies considerably according to individual taxidermists and the type of specimen they are working on. The aim is to remove the skin, ideally in one complete piece. The process generally begins with an incision that runs the length of the chest and abdomen. The skin is gently teased and peeled away from the flesh, until the body can be removed intact. Anything that will rot has to go, that is muscle, flesh, fat, eyes and brains, a process known as "fleshing out".

Once everything that can decompose has been removed, the skin is put through a series of washes to clean and preserve it. The taxidermist can then begin the process of recreating the body. Some taxidermists take precise measurements of their specimen before work begins, allowing them to craft a perfectly proportioned manikin, others work by eye. One of the most basic, and earliest methods of doing this is to make a bind-up body; this utilises wood-wool (fine wood shavings), or tow; a fine hemp fibre, that is bound up with thread to create the required shape. The skeletal structure is recreated with wire. This method is often utilised in bird taxidermy where feathers conceal muscle definition, other creatures demand a more precise recreation of the musculature. But bodies can be and are made from anything, for instance, balsa wood, fibreglass, Styrofoam, clay or papier-mâché.

There are numerous techniques that can be utilised to rebuild a specimen; mammals are skinned and nothing but the skin is utilised; everything else is removed and a replica of the

RIGHT A pair of Central American Quetzal, circa 1880, of unknown origin. The quetzal is reputed to be the most beautiful bird from the entire American continent.

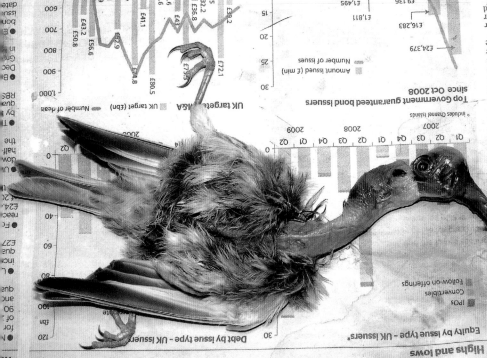

ABOVE Taxidermy is inextricably linked with death; here
a Polly Morgan finch in the process of being fleshed out.

body is built. The technique with birds is rather different; all the flesh is removed, but parts of the skeletal structure are preserved: the skull, the beak, the feet and the leg and wing bones. Reptile and fish skins are emptied but the bones of the head are not detached, simply cleaned, and the skin treated before being "re-filled"; a less common method is to take a mould and then produce a cast, painted to replicate the original. Insect body cavities are emptied, treated and then filled.

Today, pre-made manikins or forms (bodies) can be bought from taxidermy suppliers and are available in myriad sizes and poses to suit all manner of creatures, from duck to deer, piranha to python. Plastic or glass eyes, false tongues, ear-liners, or jaw sets can also be purchased to suit species and sex. A taxidermy supply catalogue makes for riveting reading.

However one chooses to recreate a specimen, working from handcrafted, precisely measured bodies or catalogue pre-made forms, once the skin is arranged around the body it is then stitched back together. This might seem to be the end of the process, but it is in fact just the start. Arguably any-one can learn the basic processes of taxidermy; it is in the setting up that the artistry comes into play.

This is a time consuming, reverential process, where every angle of the legs, wings and body is finely tuned. The expression of the eye, the minute slant of the ear, the lie of the fur, feathers, mane or crown will be worked on until the specimen is complete.

No detail is too small, for example, the damp-ness of the nose, the size of the iris, or the colour of the reproductive organs. All demand attention, even though they may be more or less hidden from view. Finally the specimen can be mounted; perhaps placed in a life-like scene where every flower and leaf has been painstakingly made from wax before being set under a dome, or set in a stark contemporary environment, bare of all decoration or even unsupported – perhaps curled up in a ball as though asleep. It may be groomed to a level of glossy perfection that it scarcely achieved in life, or sculptured to represent some grisly, ghastly fight to the death. The options are infinite.

Everyone has seen examples of bad taxidermy; cross-eyed foxes with deformed faces or menacing kittens with bulging teddy-bear eyes. Simply working with a skin does not guarantee success. Good taxidermy whether it is a blackbird on its nest, a dog holding a placard, or a dead cat, requires true artistry and a driving passion for perfection.

OVERLEAF A hunting trophy of a 11.3kg (25lb) pike from 1930. The beautifully painted piece is unusual as the pike has its prey in its mouth.

useful contacts

Animatronic Animals
www.animatronicanimals.com

This company supplies taxidermy and models of animals in either rigid fiberglass or flexible rubber or natural skin.

American Museum of Natural History (AMNH)
www.amnh.org

The AMNH in New York claims to be one of the world's pre-eminent scientific and cultural institutions with a focus on human cultures, the natural world and the universe.

Booth Museum of Natural History
194 Dyke Road, Brighton
East Sussex BN1 5AA
www.brighton-hove-rpml.org.uk.Museums/boothmuseum

A huge collection of birds and insects gathered by Victorian Edward Booth, including dioramas.

The British Historical Taxidermy Society (BHTS)
www.britishhistoricaltaxidermysociety.co.uk

The Society was formed to promote the collecting and preservation of historical taxidermy. It also encompasses research, modern taxidermy, an archive, a database and library.

Calke Abbey
Ticknall
Derby DE73 7LE
www.nationaltrust.org.uk/calke-abbey

Calke Abbey is home to a collection of taxidermy acquired by Sir Vauncey Harpur-Crew.

Department For Environment, Food And Rural affairs (DEFRA)
www.defra.gov.uk/animalhealth/cites

UK Government department for issues relating to the environment, food and rural affairs. They are responsible for issuing Specimen Specific Certificates (SSCs), valid for all commercial uses and Transaction Specific Certificates (TSCs) covering a single sale.

Deyrolle
www.deyrolle.com

Since 1831, the Deyrolle shop in Paris has offered collections of insects and shells, taxidermied animals of all kinds, curiosities from the natural world and educational materials.

The Guild of Taxidermists
www.taxidermy.org.uk

The Guild is the only officially recognised organisation actively working with the legislative authorities to secure the future for legitimate taxidermy in the UK.

The Horniman Museum
100 London Road, Forest Hill
London SE23 3PQ
www.hornimanmuseum.ac.uk

The Horniman has an acclaimed natural
history collection.

National History Museum At Tring
The Walter Rothschild Building
Akeman Street, Tring
Herfordshire HP23 6AP
www.nhm.ac.uk/tring

Home to the remarkable collections of
Walter Rothschild.

National Museum of Scotland
Chambers Street, Edinburgh
Scotland EH1 1JF
www.nms.ac.uk

The Natural World Galleries explore the evolution,
diversity and amazing abilities of animal species with a
stunning display of the best of contemporary taxidermy
alongside some very old pieces.

Natural England
www.naturalengland.org.uk/ourwork/regulation/
wildlife/licences/generallicences.aspx

A public body that aims to protect and improve
England's natural environment. It issues the
General Licences that permit the taxidermy of most
birds and mammals, excepting game and wildfowl
during the closed season.

People's Trust For Endangered Species (PTES)
www.ptes.org

PTES helps to ensure a future for many endangered
species throughout the world.

Powell-Cotton Museum
Quex House and Gardens
Quex Park, Birchington
Kent CT7 0BH
www.quexmuseum.org

A world-class natural history collection including
outstanding dioramas.

Royal Society for the Protection of Birds (RSPB)
www.rspb.org.uk

Europe's largest wildlife conservation charity.

Smithsonian Institution
www.nmh.si.edu.museums

Founded in 1846 the Smithsonian, in Washington DC,
claims to be the world's largest museum and
research complex.

ARTISTS AND TAXIDERMISTS

Bouten & Son
www.jacbouten.com/en

Founded in the Netherlands in 1918, Bouten & Son
is a renowned taxidermist. The National Museum of
Ireland, Dublin and the Museum of Scotland have
chosen Bouten & Son for restoring and mounting
their animals.

Chlöe Brown
chloeb@blueyonder.co.uk

Brown's installations incorporate sound, taxidermy
and other elements to create fantasy scenes.

Maurizio Cattelan
info@mauriziocattelanarchive.com

Italian artist based in New York, Maurizio Cattelan is
known for his challenging, tragi-comic work on themes
of death, power and authority, often utilising taxidermy.

Carl Church

www.birdtaxidermy.co.uk

Church is an international award-winning bird taxidermist.

Matthias Fahrni

www.fischpraeparation.ch

Fahrni is a two-time world champion taxidermist in the fish category.

Mike Gadd

www.taxidermy.co.uk

Gadd has over thirty years' taxidermy experience. With his great love and interest in wildlife, together with his skills as a sculptor, Mike holds an impressive portfolio.

Damien Hirst

www.damienhirst.com

One of the most influential artists of his generation, infamous for his taboo-breaking work.

David Leggett

www.wildarttaxidermy.co.uk

Leggett, of Wild Art Taxidermy, has long been recognised as one of the UK's leading practitioners, with a comprehensive range of natural history services.

Emily Mayer

emilymayer@flyingbear.co.uk

Sculptor and taxidermist Mayer is a skilled practitioner whose dark and often humorous work has challenged the more traditional notions of taxidermy.

Polly Morgan

www.pollymorgan.co.uk

Artist Polly Morgan's beautiful and macabre work is a contemporary take on the craft of taxidermy.

Joss McKinley

www.jossmckinley.com and www.mckinleyandson.co.uk

Joss McKinley is a photographer and taxidermist, He has created a collection of taxidermied birds in collaboration with Hannah Martin.

Jazmine Miles-Long

www.jazminemileslong.com

Jazmine is an ardent taxidermist, with a radical and witty approach to this controversial art form.

David Shrigley

www.davidshrigley.com

Artist David Shrigley makes wry observations on life, sometimes utilising taxidermy.

Angela Singer

www.angelasinger.com

Angela recycles taxidermy and attempts to "make the trophy more controversial, give it greater presence and make it not so easy to ignore".

bibliography

Akeley M. L. J., *Carl Akeley's Africa*, Victor Gollancz Ltd, 1931

Baillie-Grohman W. A., *Sport and Life*, Horace Cox, 1900

Browne Montagu, *Practical Taxidermy*, L. Upcott Gill, 1884

Browne Montagu, *Artistic & Scientific Taxidermy & Modelling*, Adam and Charles Black, 1896

Dance Stanley Peter, *The Art of Natural History*, Country Life Books, 1978

Madden Dave, *The Authentic Animal*, St Martin's Press, 2011

Milgrom Melissa, *Adventures in Taxidermy*, Houghton Mifflin Harcourt, 2010

Morris P. A., *A History of Taxidermy: art, science and bad taste*, MPM Publishing Ascot, 2010

Morris P. A., *Walter Potter and his Museum of Curious Taxidermy*, MPM Publishing, 2008

Moyer John W., *Practical Taxidermy*, Thames and Hudson, 1957

O'Connor P. A. *Advanced Taxidermy*, Saiga Publishing Com Ltd, 1983

Powell-Cotton Percy Horace Gordon, *In Unknown Africa: A Narrative Of Twenty Months Travel And Sport In Unknown Lands And Among New Tribes*, Hurst and Blackett, 1904

Pray L. L., *Taxidermy*, The Macmillan Company, 1945

Rothschild Miriam, *Walter Rothschild the Man the Museum and the Menagerie*, Balaban Publishers, 1983

Speake George, *Anglo-Saxon Animal Art*, Clarendon Press, 1980

Swainson W, *Taxidermy*, Longman, Brown, Green & Longmans, 1840

A *Passion for Natural History*, Edited by Clemency Fisher, National Museums & Galleries on Merseyside, 2002

picture credits